BIG PICTURE PRESS

First published in the UK in 2018 by Big Picture Press,
an imprint of Kings Road Publishing,
part of the Bonnier Publishing Group,
The Plaza, 535 King's Road, London, SW10 0SZ
www.templarco.co.uk/big-picture-press
www.bonnierpublishing.com

Illustrations copyright © 2018 by Britta Teckentrup
Text and design copyright © 2018
by Kings Road Publishing Limited

1 3 5 7 9 10 8 6 4 2

ISBN 978-1-78741-076-3

Printed in China

This book was typeset in
Core Circus Rough and Neutraface Text
The illustrations were created digitally

Written and edited by Katie Haworth
Designed by Olivia Cook

THERE ARE
FISH
EVERYWHERE

BRITTA TECKENTRUP

B P P

THERE ARE FISH EVERYWHERE

Fish live all over the world. You can find them in oceans, rivers, lakes, ponds or anywhere with enough water. They can be big or small, spiny or flat, spiky or blobby, bright or exactly the same colour as the sand, making them really hard to see. These are all fish . . . aren't they?*

Sailfish

Trumpetfish

Anchovy

Angelfish

Shark

Dolphin

Squirrelfish

Moray eel

Crab

Blenny

Starfish

Turtle

Dolphinfish

Eagle ray

Eagle ray

Royal dottyback

Seahorse

Turtle

Arapaima

Piranha

Ocean sunfish

Lionfish

Plaice

Salmon

*You're right! Some of these are NOT fish and we put them here to make sure you're still awake. Can you guess which ones are NOT fish?

IT'S A FISH!
(SO WHAT *IS* THAT?)

Fish are a type of animal that live in water. They are vertebrates, which means they have backbones. All fish have a brain and most use gills to breathe and fins to steer. They are also usually cold blooded (unable to control their body temperature) and many are covered in scales.

BONY FISH

At least 29,000 species of fish are **bony fish** – that's half of all vertebrates on the planet. These fish have a bony skeleton.

Dorsal fin

Kidney

Liver

Brain

Nostril

Swim bladder

Bony skeleton

Barbel

Caudal fin

Gills

Heart

Stomach

Anal fin

Reproductive organs

Pelvic fin

Intestine

Pectoral fin

UP AND DOWN!
(OR HOW THE SWIM BLADDER WORKS)

Many bony fish have a swim bladder – a sac filled with gas, which the fish can use to go up and down in the water.

When a fish relaxes the muscles around the swim bladder, the bladder expands and the fish rises.

When a fish tightens muscles around the swim bladder, the bladder gets smaller and the fish sinks.

IT'S NOT A FISH

Did you guess which of the creatures on the last page weren't fish?

Turtles are **reptiles**. Reptiles are cold-blooded vertebrates with dry, scaly skin. They lay their eggs on land.

Starfish (or sea stars) are **echinoderms**. Echinoderms are invertebrates (creatures without backbones) with a hard external covering.

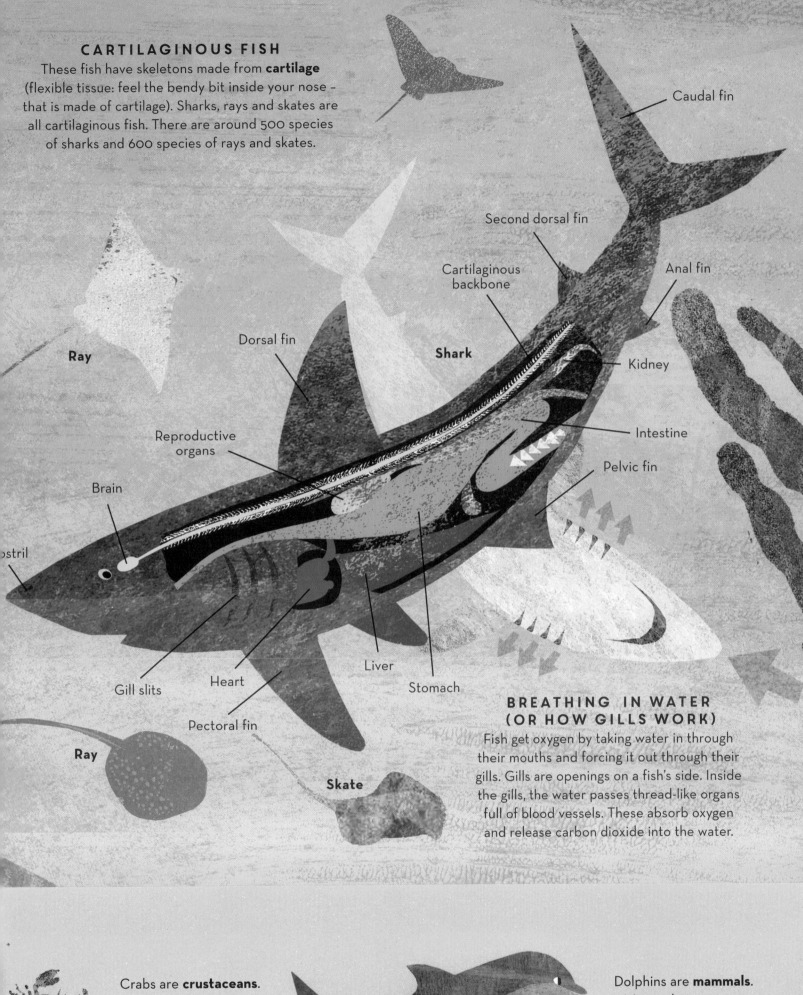

CARTILAGINOUS FISH

These fish have skeletons made from **cartilage** (flexible tissue: feel the bendy bit inside your nose – that is made of cartilage). Sharks, rays and skates are all cartilaginous fish. There are around 500 species of sharks and 600 species of rays and skates.

Caudal fin

Second dorsal fin

Cartilaginous backbone

Anal fin

Dorsal fin

Shark

Kidney

Ray

Reproductive organs

Intestine

Brain

Pelvic fin

Nostril

Gill slits

Heart

Liver

Stomach

Pectoral fin

Ray

Skate

BREATHING IN WATER (OR HOW GILLS WORK)

Fish get oxygen by taking water in through their mouths and forcing it out through their gills. Gills are openings on a fish's side. Inside the gills, the water passes thread-like organs full of blood vessels. These absorb oxygen and release carbon dioxide into the water.

Crabs are **crustaceans**. Crustaceans are invertebrates with an external skeleton in pieces (like armour) and antennae.

Dolphins are **mammals**. Mammals are warm-blooded vertebrates that feed their young with milk. (YOU are a mammal!)

FISH HAVE BEEN AROUND FOR AGES

Fish have been everywhere for a really long time. Scientists believe that there were fish on Earth for around 100 million years before animals with legs. The Devonian period (420–360 million years ago) is often called the 'Age of Fishes' because this is when some of the most important fish evolution occurred.

The very first fish we know about are the jawless fish, which first appeared around 500 million years ago. Some, like the *Hemicyclaspis*, had an armour-like outer skeleton.

Hagfish are living fossils in today's oceans. Their ancestors may have lived 500 million years ago. Hagfish produce a sticky slime to ward off predators.

500 million years ago

Hemicyclaspis

Lamprey

Hagfish

Lampreys are the only surviving jawless fish. They use their toothy mouths to attach to prey and suck blood.

'Spiny sharks' were some of the earliest jawed fish. They lived 438 to 258 million years ago and are not true sharks – they have features of both sharks and bony fishes.

The very first true shark we know much about is the **Leonodus shark**, which lived around 400 million years ago. All scientists have found to prove it existed are fossils of teeth.

Spiny shark

Leonodus shark teeth

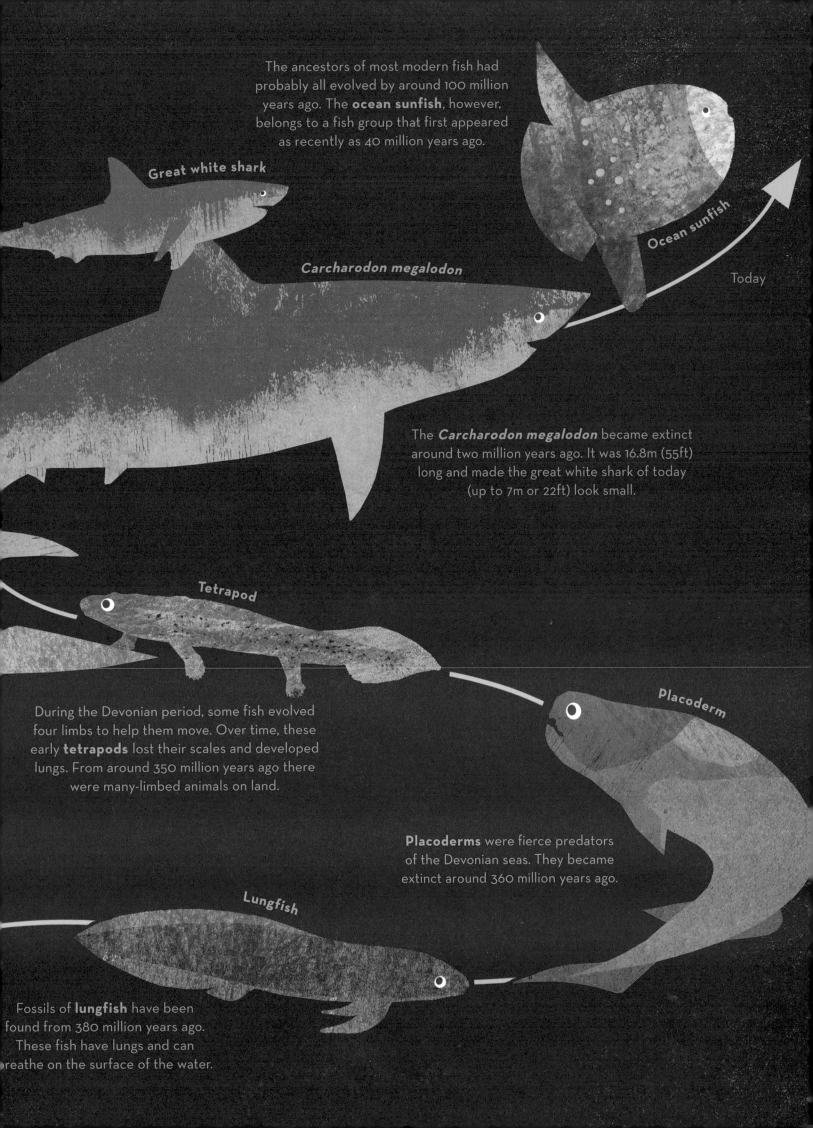

The ancestors of most modern fish had probably all evolved by around 100 million years ago. The **ocean sunfish**, however, belongs to a fish group that first appeared as recently as 40 million years ago.

Great white shark

Carcharodon megalodon

Ocean sunfish

Today

The *Carcharodon megalodon* became extinct around two million years ago. It was 16.8m (55ft) long and made the great white shark of today (up to 7m or 22ft) look small.

Tetrapod

Placoderm

During the Devonian period, some fish evolved four limbs to help them move. Over time, these early **tetrapods** lost their scales and developed lungs. From around 350 million years ago there were many-limbed animals on land.

Placoderms were fierce predators of the Devonian seas. They became extinct around 360 million years ago.

Lungfish

Fossils of **lungfish** have been found from 380 million years ago. These fish have lungs and can breathe on the surface of the water.

FRESHWATER FISH

Nearly 40 per cent of the world's fish species live in fresh water (water that isn't salty like the sea). This is despite the fact that only one per cent of the world's water is fresh. Freshwater fish live in lakes, rivers, ponds, swamps and even hot springs and caves.

Antarctica and Australia, the driest continents on Earth, have the fewest freshwater fish. Australia has over 300 native species. Antarctica has none at all (although fossils of freshwater fish have been found there that are hundreds of millions of years old).

THE AMAZON RIVER

The Amazon River begins in the Andes Mountains of South America and flows 4000km (2500mi) to the Atlantic Ocean. At the river's mouth, salt and fresh water mingle for more than 160km (100mi). The Amazon and the streams that feed it contain more than 3000 species of fish. Many migrate long distances, including the dorado catfish, which can travel 11,600km (7200mi). That's like swimming between London and New York and back again!

The **Tambaqui** eats leaves and fruit from plants near the water. Its poo spreads seeds around the Amazon rainforest.

Tambaqui

The MONSTER-sized **Arapaima** can grow more than 3m (10ft) long.

Arapaima

Red-bellied Piranha

Red-bellied Piranha can strip their prey of flesh in minutes. Their teeth are so sharp that some Amazon tribes use them as weapons.

UNEXPECTED PLACES

Some freshwater fish live in places you'd never imagine were possible.

Deserts – The Devil's Hole pupfish can only be found in one underground pool in Death Valley, Nevada – the hottest place on Earth.

On land (some of the time) – Mudskippers live in swamps and walk with their fins. They breathe through their special skin.

In caves – Mexican blind cavefish have lived underground so long that they have evolved without eyes! Being sightless helps them conserve energy.

Under ice – Circumpolar burbots live near the North Pole. They are one of the few fish to lay their eggs under ice.

The **Bull shark** is one of the few sharks that can live in salt and fresh water. They swim from the sea far up the river.

Bull shark

Dorado catfish

Dorado catfish live on the murky Amazon riverbed and use their barbels (the parts that look like a cat's whiskers) to feel their way and find food.

THE DEEP BLUE SEA

Earth is a planet covered in water. The salty oceans cover around 70 per cent of the planet's surface, and contain 97 per cent of its water. Different parts of the ocean have different types of fish – from tiny creatures darting in rock pools, to ghostly deep-sea dwellers.

THE OPEN OCEAN

OUT AT SEA, FISH ARE OFTEN LARGE, MUSCULAR AND FAST. UP TO AROUND 200M (660FT) BELOW THE SURFACE, ENOUGH LIGHT COMES THROUGH THE WATER TO ALLOW FOR PHOTOSYNTHESIS (HOW PLANTS MAKE FOOD USING THE SUN).

Anchovies swim with their mouths open to catch plankton.

Anchovies

Sleek, fast moving fish like **tuna** hunt smaller fish like anchovies.

Tuna

The **ocean sunfish** weighs up to 2300kg (5000lb) and is the heaviest bony fish.

Ocean sunfish

Zooplankton

Phytoplankton are tiny plants that live in the top 200m (660ft) of the ocean. Many fish eat them and so does **zooplankton** – very small marine animals.

Sailfish

The huge **sailfish** (up to 3.3m or 11ft long) is the world's fastest fish. It can swim at an incredible 110kph (68mph).

MARINE SHALLOWS

MANY TYPES OF FISH LIVE NEAR THE SHORE. ESTUARIES PROVIDE A SAFE PLACE FOR FISH TO LAY THEIR EGGS OR HIDE IN ROCKS.

THE TWILIGHT ZONE

BETWEEN 200M (660FT) AND 1000M (3300FT) BELOW THE SURFACE OF THE WATER IS THE TWILIGHT ZONE.

Snailfish

In 2014 scientists saw a ghostly **snailfish** at 8000m (26,000ft) in the deep Mariana Trench. Humans are only just beginning to understand the variety of life in the oceans.

The **black swallower** can swallow fish a whopping ten times its own size.

Black swallower

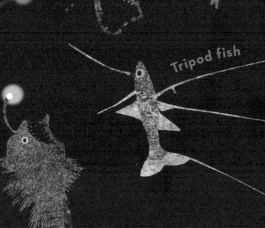

Spotted lanternfish

Many deep-sea creatures, like the **spotted lanternfish**, the **gulper eel** and the **anglerfish** make their own light by a chemical reaction called bioluminescence.

Gulper eel

Tripod fish

The **tripod fish** has long 'stilts' so it is at the perfect height for food like krill to swim into its mouth.

Anglerfish

As you go deeper, the **weight of water** increases. Deep sea fish have pressure-resistant bodies, but if they come too close to the surface, their swim bladders can expand and kill them.

DEEPER STILL

FROM 1000M (3300FT) AND DEEPER, IT IS COMPLETELY DARK. HERE FISH HAVE MADE SPECIAL ADAPTATIONS TO SURVIVE WHERE LIGHT AND FOOD ARE SCARCE.

CAN YOU FIND?

Atlantic cod lay their eggs in estuaries, but can also be found as deep as 600m (2000ft) beneath the surface. **Can you find the Atlantic cod?**

THE CORAL REEF

Beneath the ocean's warm, tropical waters, you will find colourful coral reefs. Coral reefs cover less than one per cent of Earth's surface, but around a quarter of all sea creatures live there. Put on your diving goggles and peer beneath the water – what will you see?

Yellow longn~ butterflyf~

There are around 130 species of **butterflyfish.**

Coral might look like plants, but they are animals. What looks to us like a small tree is made up of thousands of tiny creatures called polyps.

Blackback butterflyf~

Some coral use their 'arms' to catch food. Others have microscopic plants called **algae** living inside them. The algae make food for themselves and the coral.

Double-saddle butterflyfish

Layers of dead coral form **rocky reefs** on which new coral grows.

Mandarinfish smell horrible! They have poisonous spines and a smelly mucus coating to protect them from predators.

Mandarinfish

Just like a parrot, the **Pacific longnose parrotfish** has a beak. It uses it to grind coral where the algae it eats are found.

Male parrotfish

Female parrotfish

CAN YOU FIND?
Male, female and juvenile parrotfish look different. **Can you find one more of each hiding on this page?**

Juvenile parrotfish

Orange-spotted filefish

Blue Surgeonfish

Moorish Idol

Clownfish

Clownfish live near sea anemones to avoid predators. The fishes' mucus layer protects them from the anemone's sting.

Watch out for the **Blacktip reef shark** (or silvertip shark) if you're a fish! Reefs are full of food for predators like sharks and moray eels.

Hedgehog seahorse

Moray eel

FEEDING

In the world of fish, the greatest daily challenge is finding enough to eat. And fish eat a huge variety of food – everything from microscopic algae and marine creatures to . . . each other. Much of how fish behave and where they live is based on where they can find the food they need to survive.

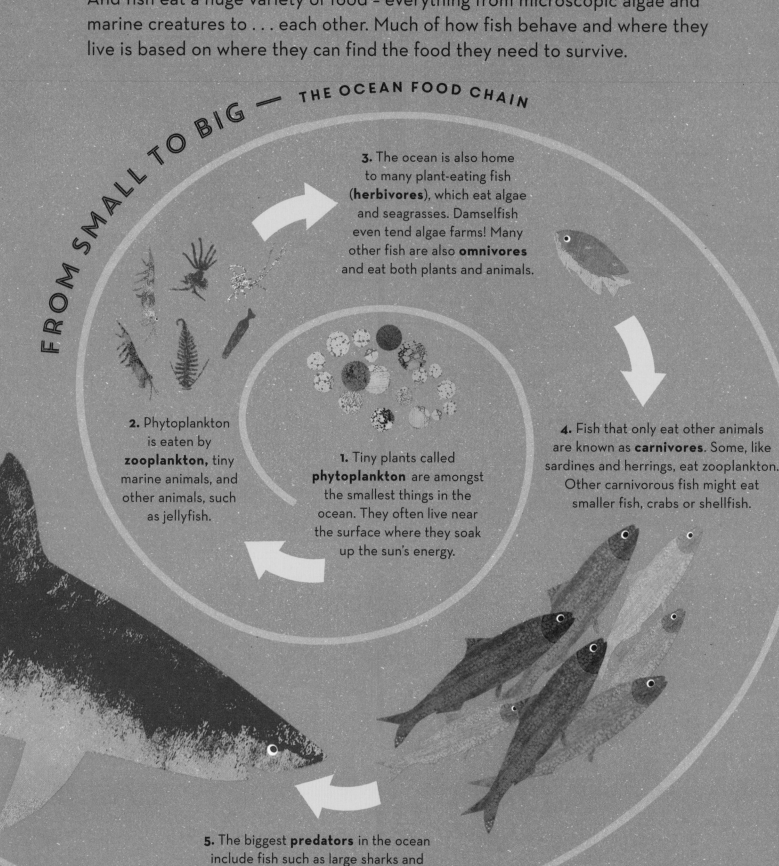

FROM SMALL TO BIG — THE OCEAN FOOD CHAIN

1. Tiny plants called **phytoplankton** are amongst the smallest things in the ocean. They often live near the surface where they soak up the sun's energy.

2. Phytoplankton is eaten by **zooplankton,** tiny marine animals, and other animals, such as jellyfish.

3. The ocean is also home to many plant-eating fish (**herbivores**), which eat algae and seagrasses. Damselfish even tend algae farms! Many other fish are also **omnivores** and eat both plants and animals.

4. Fish that only eat other animals are known as **carnivores**. Some, like sardines and herrings, eat zooplankton. Other carnivorous fish might eat smaller fish, crabs or shellfish.

5. The biggest **predators** in the ocean include fish such as large sharks and tuna, mammals such as dolphins and seals, and birds such as penguins.

WEIRD AND WONDERFUL FEEDERS

Meet some of the fish world's most innovative eaters.

Unlike humans, fish don't just have taste buds on their tongues. They can be on their faces or all over their bodies. **Catfish** have up to 175,000 taste buds (humans have around 10,000). Most are on their barbels – the fleshy feelers that look like a cat's whiskers.

Catfish

Archerfish

Archerfish know how to spit! They spit a powerful jet of water at insects to bring them down into the water.

Sharks have cells on their heads that can detect electric fields. This is called 'electroreception'.

Shark

The largest fish in the ocean eats some of the smallest food! **Whale Sharks** (12m or 40ft long) prefer to eat tiny plankton, which they filter out of the water they suck into their huge mouths.

Whale shark

Anglerfish dangle a 'lure' in the water to attract prey, just like human fishermen. This lure is a special light organ on the fish's head.

Anglerfish

Electric eel

Electric eels stun their prey with an electric shock of up to 600 volts.

STAYING ALIVE

Underwater, it's a fish-eat-fish world. Smaller, weaker fish are constantly threatened by hungry predators. Many have evolved amazing ways to avoid being eaten – from simply becoming very good at hiding to forming surprising relationships with other creatures.

CAN YOU FIND?

Some fish have adapted to look exactly like their environments. Can you find these masters of disguise?

Leaf scorpionfish

Largetooth flounder

Yellow crested weedfish

Leafy seadragon

Stonefish*

*Be careful! This is one of the most poisonous fish on Earth!

MASTERS OF SURVIVAL

sh don't just rely on camouflage. There are
any other ways they have learned to survive.

MAKING EYES
Some small fish, like the
damselfish develop an eye-
shaped marking on their fins. This
confuses larger fish, as it looks
like the damselfish are swimming
in the opposite direction.

CHEMICAL WEAPONS
When it is threatened, the **whitespotted
boxfish** releases a poison that is strong
enough to kill other fish.

I'M BIGGER THAN YOU THOUGHT!
Spotted porcupinefish have a special escape tactic.
If they are threatened by a predator they can fill their
stomachs with water, puff up to more than twice as large
as they were and extend their fierce spines.

Before

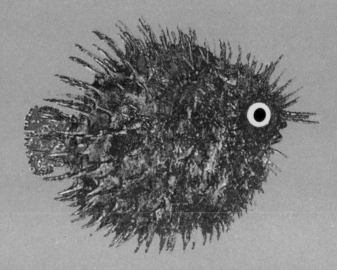

After

TRAVELLING COMPANIONS
Some fish develop special relationships
with toxic sea anemones or jellyfish to keep
predators at bay. Juvenile **golden trevally** can
often be found in jellyfish tentacles.

HIDE-AND-SEEK
Many fish hide in rocks, plants or reefs.
Squirrelfish hide during the day and
come out at night. They make clicking,
grunting noises to scare off predators.

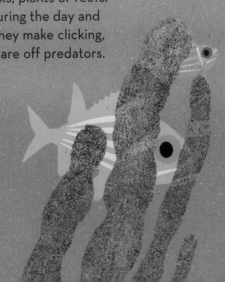

SCHOOLING

Another way fish avoid predators is by swimming in schools. What is a school of fish? (And no, it's not where fish learn maths.) A school is a group of fish that all swim together in the same direction and in a tight formation.

Fish swim in schools to **confuse predators**. A moving mass of fish looks like a bigger creature and makes it hard for a predator to single out its prey.

Fish swimming at the back need **less energy** to swim because they are helped by water movement made by the fish at the front.

Indian mimic goatfish

CAN YOU FIND?
Although the Indian mimic goatfish looks like a bluestripe snapper, it is not! These fish often school with bluestripe snapper to hide from predators. **Can you find all the goatfish in this school?**

Bluestripe snapper

Bluestripe snapper are found in tropical waters. They school near reefs, caves and shipwrecks. Fish usually school with fish from the same species. They recognise each other by their scent.

Hungry fish may swim at the front or on the outsides of the school, even though this is more dangerous. It is easier to find food from this position.

Scientists have discovered that fish with **speedy reaction times** are more likely to lead a school.

Schools of fish can **change direction quickly** to avoid predators.

FISH PARENTS

There are all sorts of ways that fish mate, lay their eggs and care for the next generation. Many fish lay eggs that are fertilised outside their bodies, but some give birth to live young. Some fish let their eggs drift in the tide, while others build elaborate nests, which they defend aggressively. Fish parents have adapted to give the next generation the best chance of survival.

RAISING THE ODDS

Many fish that live in the open ocean 'spawn'. Spawning is when female fish release eggs into the water and they are fertilised outside the fishes' bodies by males. Every year billions of **sardines** gather in a huge school near South Africa to spawn. Sardine eggs drift in the ocean and parents do not care for their young.

ELABORATE COURTSHIP

Some fish have elaborate courtship rituals. This **Japanese pufferfish** is thought to create an incredible pattern in the sand to attract a mate.

HE TO SHE

Some fish even change sex as part of the mating process. **Clownfish** are all born male and live in groups with one dominant female. When she dies, a male will change to a female to take her place.

MOUTH NURSERY

Some female **African cichlids** keep their eggs in their mouth for up to 36 days. Young fish will still seek protection in their mother's mouth.

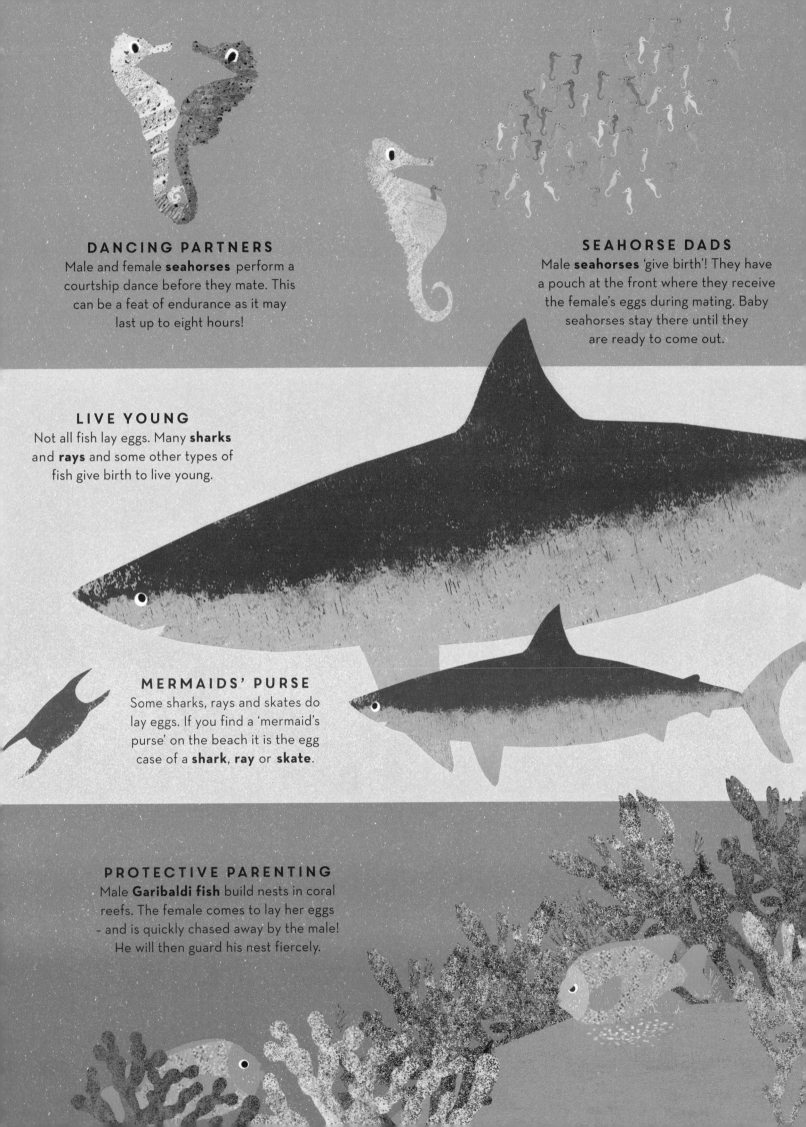

DANCING PARTNERS

Male and female **seahorses** perform a courtship dance before they mate. This can be a feat of endurance as it may last up to eight hours!

SEAHORSE DADS

Male **seahorses** 'give birth'! They have a pouch at the front where they receive the female's eggs during mating. Baby seahorses stay there until they are ready to come out.

LIVE YOUNG

Not all fish lay eggs. Many **sharks** and **rays** and some other types of fish give birth to live young.

MERMAIDS' PURSE

Some sharks, rays and skates do lay eggs. If you find a 'mermaid's purse' on the beach it is the egg case of a **shark**, **ray** or **skate**.

PROTECTIVE PARENTING

Male **Garibaldi fish** build nests in coral reefs. The female comes to lay her eggs - and is quickly chased away by the male! He will then guard his nest fiercely.

ATLANTIC SALMON

Atlantic salmon go to great lengths to breed – literally! They may migrate many thousands of miles. Adult salmon live in the freezing waters of the North Atlantic Ocean near Greenland. After one to four years at sea they return to the rivers where they were born in Europe, North America and Russia. Here they lay their eggs. Young salmon return to the sea and the cycle begins all over again.

Male salmon turn orange and their heads change shape.

Breeding female

Breeding male

Female salmon become dark green with blue and purple colours on their sides.

Salmon enter rivers between **April and November**. At this point they begin to look very different and they stop eating.

Adult salmon

Adult salmon are silvery grey. At sea they feed on small fish.

CAN YOU FIND
all the predators looking for salmon to eat?

manage to swim back to the rivers where they were born. Scientists believe they navigate by **magnetic fields** and the **stars** while at sea and by **smell** and **taste** in rivers.

Newly hatched fish are called **alevins.**

The **eggs** are fertilised by males as they are released.

When salmon reach the area they were born in, between **October and January**, they lay their eggs. Female salmon bury their eggs in riverbed gravel.

Once the alevins have absorbed the yolk sacs that protrude from their bodies, they are known as **fry.**

By the end of summer the fish are around 4cm (1.6in) long with dark markings. These are called **parr.**

After two or three years, the parr change colour. These small, silvery salmon are called **smolts**. In spring smolts swim downriver to the sea.

Alevin

Fry

Parr

Eggs

Smolt

FISH AND PEOPLE

Fish have been an important source of food for humans for thousands of years. Many people are also fascinated by the behaviour of fish or prize them for their beautiful colours. And now, scientists are seeking new species thousands of metres beneath the ocean's surface.

ICE FISHING
Some cultures have developed ways of **fishing** in even the most hostile environments. The Inuit people of Alaska and Canada catch fish through holes in the ice during winter.

FISHING TACKLE
Early humans had to develop technology to catch fish. The earliest **fish hooks** found so far come from the island of Okinawa in Japan and the oldest could be as much as 23,000 years old.

PRETTY PETS
Have you ever had a **goldfish**? Keeping goldfish as pets was common amongst wealthy people in ninth-century China.

ANCIENT RECIPE
The city of Pompeii in ancient Rome was famous for making, **garum**, a fish sauce that was very popular. To make garum, mash together fish with their eggs and entrails. Then leave the mixture for six weeks until it has fermented. Yum!

PROTECTED PLACES

A **marine reserve** is part of the ocean where fishing is not allowed and where the natural environment is protected. The largest marine reserve is in Antarctica's Ross Sea. Fish, penguins, wales and other creatures go there to feed on krill.

TAKING TOO MUCH?

The world's biggest fishing trawler can catch 400 tons (360 million metric tons) of fish in 24 hours. Some species have been greatly reduced by commercial methods like this, including **dolphins** and **turtles**, which are thrown away because they cannot be sold.

PLASTIC SOUP

Do you really need a straw with your drink? Plastic items like this end up in our oceans and are **endangering marine life**. More than 12 million tons (11 million metric tons) may be added to the ocean every year. You can help by reducing the amount of plastic you use and by recycling.

NEW LIFE?

New species of marine animals are discovered every year. Scientists exploring the Mariana Trench, the deepest place in the ocean, use special robots like the *Nereus* to find what lives in the deep.

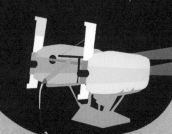